Demetrio Says "No"

Based on a true story about a little boy
who refused to take off his jacket

Linda Griffin

Illustrated by Jill Dubin

Griffinbooks.net

This book is dedicated, with much love and admiration,
to my brother Richard and niece Iliana.

This is Demetrio.

He's usually a cheerful little boy who likes to go to school, but this morning he walked into his kindergarten classroom feeling unhappy.

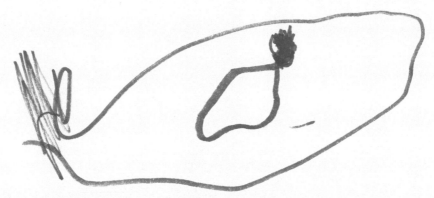

All the boys and girls sat at their tables. They had to take turns hanging up their coats in a small closet.

"Table one, hang up your clothing," Miss Bliss said in a pleasant voice.

The children walked to the closet to put away their jackets and sweaters.

This time, Miss Bliss held up a sign that said "two."

All the children at table two started to put away their things – all except Demetrio.

He just sat.

Miss Bliss walked over to Demetrio and showed him the sign.

"Do you remember what this says?" Miss Bliss asked.

Demetrio did not say a word. He just sat with his head down and chin on his chest. His jacket remained zipped up tight.

"It's time to hang up your clothing."

Demetrio did not move from his seat.

All the boys and girls looked at Demetrio. Then they looked at Miss Bliss.

"It's warm in here, but you may hang up your jacket when you're ready," Miss Bliss said.

The children did their jobs, fixed the calendar and read the plan for the day."

Demetrio didn't take off his jacket.

The children had their snack.

Demetrio still didn't take off his jacket.

Miss Bliss walked over to Demetrio.

"I bet you're wearing something you don't like," Miss Bliss said.

"Let me guess."

"Your shirt has holes in it like a piece of Swiss cheese."

Demetrio shook his head. "No," he said.

"You spilled chocolate milk down the center of the shirt and it looks like you have an octopus on the front."

Demetrio shook his head. "No," he said.

"Then it must be the color of green slime!"

A faint smile appeared on Demetrio's face as he shook his head. "No," he said again.

"Yucky brown, then."

Demetrio shook his head. "No," he said, even louder.

"Well then, what color is it?"

"Blue," Demetrio said, smiling.

"Blue?" Miss Bliss asked.

Demetrio started to laugh. "My mommy made me wear it. It's ugly!"

"You certainly don't like that shirt," Miss Bliss said.

Miss Bliss called the children for the next reading
group. Demetrio came with his workbook and pencil.

He was still wearing his jacket and underneath it was his ugly blue shirt.

As soon as Demetrio came home from school, he took off his ugly blue shirt and hid it.

Where do you think he put it?

Demetrio won't tell.

Draw a picture of where you think Demetrio hid his shirt.

To Foster Comprehension, Conversation and Creativity

(Discuss two or three questions. Save the rest for future readings.)

Before Reading The Story

Did you ever refuse to do something your teacher asked? Share your experience.

What happened when a classmate didn't do what the teacher asked?

Discuss feelings, fairness, and alternatives to the actions of teacher and child.

During The Story

Why do you think Demetrio won't take off his jacket?

What do you think the teacher will do?

Do you think Demetrio will eventually take off his jacket?

Why or why not?

After The Story Has Been Read

What would you have done if you were Demetrio?

What would you have done if you were the teacher?

Read the story again and take turns changing the ending of the story.

Draw a picture of where you think Demetrio hid his shirt.

Other Books By Linda Griffin, MS

My Child Won't Listen ... and other early childhood problems

This is a book for parents, educators and other professionals who work with young children and want strategies that work.

Adopting Ginger

This award-winning picture book is about Ginger's journey from a shelter to a loving home. *Adopting Ginger* is a story about compassion, cooperation and responsibility.

Listening level ages 5 and up
Reading level ages 8 – 12 and dog lovers of all ages

Books can be ordered on Amazon.com or BarnesandNoble.com

98083443R00021

Made in the USA
Lexington, KY
04 September 2018